WOMEN in the ARTS

By Rebecca Phillips-Bartlett

Minneapolis, Minnesota

Credits

All images are courtesy of Shutterstock.com, unless otherwise specified. With thanks to Getty Images, Thinkstock Photo, and iStockphoto. Cover – balabolka, Amma Shams. Throughout – balabolka, Amma Shams. 4–5 – PeopleImages.com - Yuri A. 6–7 – AnonymousUnknown author, Public domain, via Wikimedia Commons, Suzuki Harunobu, Public domain, via Wikimedia Commons, Takashi Images, Orfeev. 8–9 – National Portrait Gallery (United States), Public domain, via Wikimedia Commons, Edmonia Lewis, Public domain, via Wikimedia Commons, Unknown photographer, Public domain, via Wikimedia Commons, Dari-designPie, In Art. 10–11 – Apeda Studio New York, Public domain, via Wikimedia Commons, Marcellin Auzolle, Public domain, via Wikimedia Commons, Alice Guy-Blaché, Public domain, via Wikimedia Commons, Film Fun, January 1918, Public domain, via Wikimedia Commons, Alice Guy, Public domain, via Wikimedia Commons, Cobisimo, ginanperdana - nantachi, antishock, hans sitompul. 12–13 – Foto: Rothschild Photo Los Angeles, Public domain, via Wikimedia Commons, New Africa, 4zevar, lena__nikolaeva, Polina Tomtosova, Anna Shalygina. 14–15 – The original uploader was ImpuMozhi at English Wikipedia, Public domain, via Wikimedia Commons, Post of India, GODL-India <https://data.gov.in/sites/default/files/Gazette__Notification__OGDL.pdf>, via Wikimedia Commons, JN STUDIO, ideyweb, Darvik Design. 16–17 – Guillermo Kahlo, Public domain, via Wikimedia Commons, Editor Itesm A01335798, CC BY-SA 4.0 <https://creativecommons.org/licenses/by-sa/4.0>, via Wikimedia Commons, Ambra75, CC BY-SA 4.0 <https://creativecommons.org/licenses/by-sa/4.0>, via Wikimedia Commons, Panuwach, Glinskaja Olga. 18–19 – Per Olov Jansson via Wikimedia Commons, Maris Grunskis, Olga Popova, Elizaveta Melentyeva, Yana Alisovna, Minur. 20–21 – kyle tsui from Washington, DC, USA, CC BY 2.0 <https://creativecommons.org/licenses/by/2.0>, via Wikimedia Commons, Office of the White House, Public domain, via Wikimedia Commons, Iconic Bestiary, GulArt, CreativeChamber. 22–23 – Maria Starus, Zlatko Guzmic, Kathy Hutchins, David7, kichikimi. 24–25 – Dmitry Ternovoy, FAL, via Wikimedia Commons, Peeradontax, mhatzapa, David Burrows, Antlii. 26–27 – Kathy Hutchins, LEE SNIDER PHOTO IMAGES, Devita ayu silvianingtyas, DandelionFly, Alona Savchuk, Bilbo Baggins, Abramova Aleksandra. 28–29 – Richard Rothwell, Public domain, via Wikimedia Commons, Cecilio Ricardo, U.S. Air Force, Public domain, via Wikimedia Commons, lev radin, Chairman of the Joint Chiefs of Staff from Washington D.C., United States, CC BY 2.0 <https://creativecommons.org/licenses/by/2.0>, via Wikimedia Commons, Logonv.

Bearport Publishing Company Product Development Team
President: Jen Jenson; Director of Product Development: Spencer Brinker; Managing Editor: Allison Juda; Associate Editor: Naomi Reich; Associate Editor: Tiana Tran; Art Director: Colin O'Dea; Designer: Kim Jones; Designer: Kayla Eggert; Product Development Assistant: Owen Hamlin

Library of Congress Cataloging-in-Publication Data is available at www.loc.gov or upon request from the publisher.

ISBN: 979-8-88916-979-6 (hardcover)
ISBN: 979-8-89232-511-0 (paperback)
ISBN: 979-8-89232-163-1 (ebook)

© 2025 BookLife Publishing
This edition is published by arrangement with BookLife Publishing.

North American adaptations © 2025 Bearport Publishing Company. All rights reserved. No part of this publication may be reproduced in whole or in part, stored in any retrieval system, or transmitted in any form or by any means, electronic, mechanical, photocopying, recording, or otherwise, without written permission from the publisher. Bearport Publishing is a division of Chrysalis Education Group.

For more information, write to Bearport Publishing, 5357 Penn Avenue South, Minneapolis, MN 55419.

Contents

She Who Dares 4
Murasaki Shikibu 6
Edmonia Lewis 8
Alice Guy-Blaché 10
Edith Head 12
Rukmini Devi Arundale 14
Frida Kahlo 16
Tove Jansson 18
Maya Angelou 20
Dolly Parton 22
Zaha Hadid 24
Laverne Cox 26

More Daring Women 28
Changing the World 30
Glossary 31
Index 32
Read More 32
Learn More Online 32

She Who Dares

Many people are creative and enjoy making beautiful works of art. Art can be paintings and drawings. But it can also take the form of music, dance, **literature**, movies, fashion, and even **architecture**. Art is all around us!

There are many reasons people choose to create art. Some people use art as an escape from the troubles in their lives, while others create art to tell stories or convey important messages. No matter the reason, people use art to express themselves.

Showing the world who you are is important. How do you express yourself?

THE WORK OF WONDERFUL WOMEN

Women have interesting and amazing lives with their own stories to tell. Throughout history, many women have turned to art to create incredible things and show the world their talents.

However, it has not always been easy for women in the arts. Many daring women have had to break through **barriers**. But they have found strength in their creativity. Some women even use their art to help others.

Breaking through barriers takes lots of bravery and courage.

How do you find strength when you are facing a challenge?

5

Murasaki Shikibu

AMAZING AUTHOR

Born: Around 978 CE   **Died:** Around 1014 CE

Murasaki Shikibu was born in Kyōto, Japan. Because her family was rich, Shikibu was allowed to learn things that were usually taught only to boys. She studied many languages and learned to write beautiful poems.

Shikibu's poems were so good that she was offered a job working for the empress of Japan. She used her language skills to teach the empress Chinese poetry.

As well as writing poems, Shikibu kept a diary.

While Shikibu was working for the empress, she learned a lot about the lives of the Japanese nobility. She used this knowledge to write a story. Shikibu's story is thought to be the world's very first novel!

Shikibu's story included some poems.

Murasaki Shikibu was not actually this author's name. It is the name of a character in her novel. The writer's real name is lost to time.

Edmonia Lewis

SPEAKING THROUGH SCULPTURES

Born: 1844   **Died:** 1907

Edmonia Lewis was born in Greenbush, New York. Her parents died when she was young, so she lived with her aunts among **Indigenous** Americans. Lewis's older brother paid for her to go to school, which was a rare opportunity for a woman at the time. She studied at Oberlin College. However, because of racist attitudes, she was forced to leave the school before she could graduate.

Lewis was biracial. She was both Black and Native American.

Eventually, Lewis moved to Boston, Massachusetts. There, she met a successful sculptor named Edward Brackett. He taught Lewis sculpting and helped her set up a workspace of her own.

Edward Brackett

8

Lewis started sculpting with clay and plaster. She created small sculptures of famous **abolitionists**. Then, she began creating larger pieces. Lewis sold her sculptures and used the money to move to Rome, Italy. Even though most sculptors in Rome paid other people to work on parts of their pieces, Lewis did all her own work.

One of Lewis's most famous sculptures is called *Forever Free*. It shows two people being freed from slavery.

Lewis became very successful. She was the first Black American who was a paid sculptor.

Lewis was called Wildfire among her Indigenous family.

Alice Guy-Blaché

A FIRST IN FILM

Born: 1873   **Died:** 1968

Alice Guy-Blaché was born in Paris, France. In 1894, she worked as a secretary for Léon Gaumont, an inventor who created an early kind of movie camera. Guy-Blaché learned a lot about cameras and even helped take photographs.

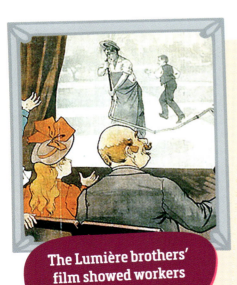

The Lumière brothers' film showed workers leaving a factory.

In 1895, Guy-Blaché and Gaumont were invited to see the first film made by the Lumière brothers. The brothers used their own movie camera to tell stories about real-life events. Guy-Blaché liked their films but knew there was a way to make them even better. She asked Gaumont if she could use one of his cameras to tell stories about fictional worlds.

10

In 1896, Guy-Blaché created the first film with a completely fictional story and setting. Her film, called *The Cabbage Fairy*, was less than a minute long, but it showed that cameras could be used to bring one's imagination to the screen. Guy-Blaché continued to prove this as she went on to make hundreds of films.

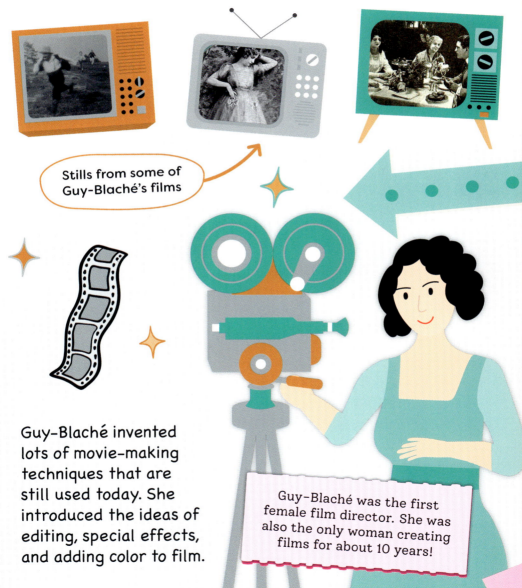

Stills from some of Guy-Blaché's films

Guy-Blaché invented lots of movie-making techniques that are still used today. She introduced the ideas of editing, special effects, and adding color to film.

Guy-Blaché was the first female film director. She was also the only woman creating films for about 10 years!

Edith Head

COSTUME CREATOR

Born: 1897 **Died:** 1981

Edith Head was born in San Bernardino, California. She taught foreign languages as a schoolteacher and studied art at an evening class. In 1923, Head was struggling with money, so she applied for a job as a costume sketch artist at a film studio.

Head arrived at the studio with lots of sketches. She was hired on the spot! After getting the job, Head admitted that she had borrowed many of the drawings from her classmates. However, the studio was starting to make international films. So, Head's language skills would prove valuable, and she kept her job.

Drawing a sketch is often one of the first steps for a costume designer.

During the next year, Head learned how to design costumes for movies. In 1925, she got her first opportunity to design costumes for characters with smaller roles. A couple of years later, she was creating costumes for huge Hollywood stars!

The first costume Head designed was covered in real chocolate! Unfortunately, the chocolate melted under the hot studio lights.

Head worked hard and became the chief designer at a huge film studio. During her life, she won eight Academy Awards for Best Costume Design. This is more than any other person in history. Head is remembered as one of the greatest costume designers in film.

Head wore dark glasses to help her see what costumes would look like in black-and-white films. It became part of her signature look!

Rukmini Devi Arundale

DARING DANCER

Born: 1904   **Died:** 1986

Rukmini Devi Arundale was born in Tamil Nadu, India. Her family followed a spiritual way of thinking called theosophy. This helped encourage her belief that people were more than their social status.

In 1928, Arundale met a ballet dancer named Anna Pavlova. This was the beginning of her passion for dance. Pavlova encouraged Arundale to learn **traditional** Indian dance styles. Arundale learned a dance called Bharatanatyam (baa-ruhh-taa-NAA-tee-uhm). At the time, Bharatanatyam was not very well respected.

Arundale was about 30 years old when she started dancing.

In 1935, Arundale performed Bharatanatyam at a public event. It got people interested in the traditional dance. Then, she started a group called the Kalakshetra **Foundation**, which focused on keeping traditional Indian art styles alive. Arundale and her foundation changed people's attitudes toward Bharatanatyam. It has become a popular and well-respected style of dance.

A Bharatanatyam dancer

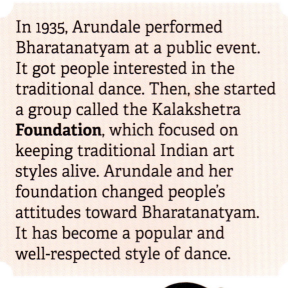

Arundale created more than 25 Bharatanatyam dance dramas.

Arundale was also very involved in politics. She was one of the first women to be part of India's **parliament**. Part of her political work helped set up India's Animal Welfare Board, which works to keep animals safe.

15

Frida Kahlo

PAINTING THROUGH HER PAIN

Born: 1907   **Died:** 1954

Frida Kahlo was born in Mexico City, Mexico. When she was six years old, Kahlo became very sick with a virus called polio. She wasn't able to leave her bed for nine months, and her right leg was injured for life.

Kahlo's home was called the Blue House. Today, the house is a museum about her life and art.

When she was about 18 years old, Kahlo was in a bus crash. She suffered a terrible injury that kept her in the hospital for a long time. While recovering, she started painting **self-portraits**. Kahlo used her paintings to express how she was feeling.

16

Kahlo's painting called *Self-Portrait with Monkeys*

Kahlo's paintings are often thought of as **surrealist** because they have a dreamlike quality. However, Kahlo told people that she painted her real life and pain, not her dreams.

In many of her works, Kahlo painted herself wearing traditional Mexican clothes with bright colors. She is remembered for her celebration of Mexican culture and the representation of her experience as a Mexican woman.

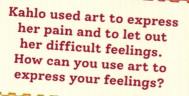

Kahlo used art to express her pain and to let out her difficult feelings. How can you use art to express your feelings?

17

Tove Jansson

IMAGINING INCREDIBLE ILLUSTRATIONS

Born: 1914   **Died:** 2001

Tove Jansson was born in Helsinki, Finland. Her family was very artistic. As a child, Jansson spent many summers surrounded by nature on distant islands. Nature and art were important parts of her life.

By the age of seven, Jansson was writing and **illustrating** her own stories. As an adult, she started selling her illustrations to a political magazine. But during World War II (1939–1945), Jansson wanted an escape from politics. She turned to her childhood memories and created the world of the Moomins.

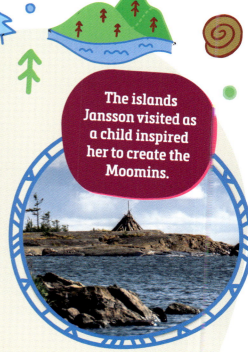

The islands Jansson visited as a child inspired her to create the Moomins.

18

The Moomins were troll characters who went on little adventures. In 1945, Jansson's first story about the Moomins was **published**. She went on to create more novels, picture books, and comic strips about the trolls. Her stories have been **translated** into more than 50 languages so that children around the world can read them.

The Moomins on Finnish postage stamps

When she was almost 50 years old, Jansson and her partner built a cabin on a tiny island. The island had no electricity or running water, but the pair spent their summers there for many years.

In 1966, Jansson was awarded the Hans Christian Andersen Medal for her work in children's literature.

Maya Angelou

ASTONISHING AUTOBIOGRAPHIES

Born: 1928   **Died:** 2014

Maya Angelou was born in St. Louis, Missouri. When she was young, Angelou's parents split up and sent her to live with her grandmother. At age seven, Angelou was attacked. This had such a big effect on her that she stopped speaking for years. During this time, her love of reading and writing grew. It eventually gave her the courage to speak again.

In her 20s, Angelou worked as a singer, a dancer, and an actress.

As a teenager, Angelou moved to San Francisco, California. She got a job as a streetcar conductor. She was likely the first Black American woman in the city to have this job.

20

In 1959, Angelou moved to New York City and joined a writing group called the Harlem Writers Guild. This was a group of Black American authors who worked to encourage and help others get their writing published.

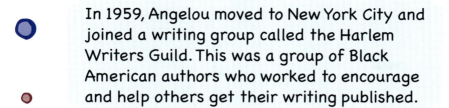

President Barack Obama awarded Angelou the Presidential Medal of Freedom.

Angelou worked on her writing and published her first **autobiography** in 1969. She wrote about the strength that helped her overcome her childhood struggles. More than a million copies of her book have been sold, and it has never gone out of print.

Imagine you are writing an autobiography. What have been the most interesting parts of your life to include?

Dolly Parton

SINGING HER STORY

Born: 1946

Dolly Parton was born in Locust Ridge, Tennessee. She grew up in a poor family with 11 siblings. They all lived in a one-room cabin. Parton's family may not have had a lot of money, but they always had music. Parton learned many songs from her mom and began performing at church.

A Tennessee mountain cabin similar to Parton's childhood home

When Parton was young, her uncle bought her a guitar. Soon, she was was writing her own songs and singing them on the porch of her cabin. Parton's uncle helped her get spots performing on local TV and radio shows when she was just 10 years old.

After finishing high school, Parton moved to Nashville, Tennessee, to work on her music career. She became part of a duo with a famous country singer named Porter Wagoner. Parton was a rising star, and she soon started her solo career.

Dolly Parton has two stars on the Hollywood Walk of Fame.

Parton has won many awards and changed the world of country music. She has also worked hard to improve the lives of other people. In 1988, Parton set up the Dollywood Foundation to help pay for education for children who live near where she grew up.

Many of Parton's songs are about her life and about growing up in **poverty**.

Parton wants every child to have their own books. She started a program called Dolly Parton's Imagination Library, which sends millions of books to children every year.

23

Zaha Hadid

BREATHTAKING BUILDINGS

Born: 1950 **Died:** 2016

Zaha Hadid was born in Baghdad, Iraq. She studied math at college. After she finished school, Hadid moved to London, England, to study architecture. Architecture uses lots of math to design beautiful buildings.

Vitra Fire Station was Hadid's first major building.

At first, Hadid was told that her designs were too complicated to actually build. Even though many people said her plans would never be possible, Hadid worked hard to make her designs a reality.

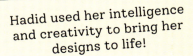

Hadid used her intelligence and creativity to bring her designs to life!

Hadid continued to make incredible designs. She experimented with space and angles to create buildings that would stand out from others.

Hadid designed the London Aquatic Center for the 2012 Olympic Games.

In 2004, Hadid was the first woman to win the Pritzker Architecture Prize. She worked hard and had become a very well-known and respected architect.

25

Laverne Cox

ACTIVIST ACTRESS

Born: 1972

Laverne Cox was born in Mobile, Alabama. She and her twin brother lived with their mom. Cox is **transgender**. Everyone thought that she was a boy when she was born. However, Cox always knew that she was not.

As a child, Cox loved to perform. She begged her mother to let her learn to dance. She was an amazing dancer and continued to study dance at college. Cox also joined theater groups and started acting.

Once she finished school, Cox spent years trying to get acting jobs. She made hundreds of postcards with her information and sent them to different directors. Eventually, she was offered her first job on a TV show!

Since then, Cox has acted in many shows. She even became the first openly transgender person to be **nominated** for an Emmy Award in acting. Cox uses her success to speak out about human rights. She has written essays and films about transgender people's lives and experiences.

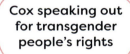

Cox speaking out for transgender people's rights

More Daring Women

MARY WOLLSTONECRAFT SHELLEY and Her Scary Stories

Born: 1797   **Died:** 1851

During a stormy summer, Mary Wollstonecraft Shelley and her friends had a ghost story competition. One night, Shelley had a very bad dream. This inspired her novel *Frankenstein*, the famous book about a scientist who creates a monster. It is now thought of as one of the first science fiction stories.

Many other artists have used Shelley's monster in their own stories.

ARETHA FRANKLIN and Her Soulful Songs

Born: 1942   **Died:** 2018

As a girl, Aretha Franklin taught herself to play the piano and sing. By the age of 14, she was recording her first songs. Franklin became famous and was often called the Queen of Soul. She used her success to get involved in the civil rights movement and fight for Black people's rights.

MAYA LIN and Her Celebrated Sculptures

Born: 1959

Maya Lin studied architecture at college. Her first big break came when she won a competition to design a war memorial. Her design was simple, which was very different from other memorials. Lin has continued to create powerful political sculptures.

AMANDA S. C. GORMAN and Her Powerful Poetry

Born: 1998

Gorman has written several books.

Amanda S. C. Gorman had a **speech impediment** when she was young. She used music and poetry to teach herself how to say certain sounds. In 2021, Gorman became the youngest person to perform their poem at a president's **inauguration**.

Changing the World

Many women have used art to share different stories with the world. Whether they were making political points, coming up with revolutionary ideas, or **empowering** others, the world would not be the same without women in the arts!

These women had the strength to overcome challenges and break through difficult barriers. They dared to be different so they could change the world.

Many artists create things that are inspired by their real lives. What inspires you?

DO YOU DARE TO CHANGE THE WORLD?

Glossary

abolitionists people who worked to end slavery

architecture a style or method of building design

autobiography a book someone writes about their own life

barriers obstacles that block or limit access to something

empowering giving the confidence to do things or make decisions

foundation a group that supports or gives money to certain causes

illustrating drawing pictures

inauguration the swearing-in ceremony that marks the beginning of a president's term of office

Indigenous people that originally lived and may continue to live in a certain place

literature written works that have lasting importance or interest

nominated chosen to be considered for an award

parliament a group of people who have been elected to make laws in some countries

poverty the state of being very poor

published printed and released for people to read

self-portraits paintings or drawings of an artist that are done by the artist themself

speech impediment a condition that makes it difficult to speak clearly

surrealist having to do with a kind of art that has dreamlike qualities

traditional having stayed the same for many years

transgender someone whose gender identity is different from what they were assigned at birth

translated made into a different language than the original

INDEX

actress 20, 26
Angelou, Maya 20–21
Arundale, Rukmini Devi 14–15
awards 13, 19, 21, 23, 27
books 19, 21, 23, 28–29
buildings 24–25
Cox, Laverne 26–27
dance 4, 14–15, 20, 26
empress 6–7
films 10–13, 27
foundation 15, 23
Franklin, Aretha 28
Gorman, Amanda S.C. 29
Guy-Blaché, Alice 10–11
Hadid, Zaha 24–25
Head, Edith 12–13
Jansson, Tove 18–19
Kahlo, Frida 16–17
Lewis, Edmonia 8–9
Lin, Maya 29
novels 7, 19, 28
paintings 4, 16–17
Parton, Dolly 22–23
poems 6–7, 29
sculptures 8–9, 29
Shelley, Mary Wollstonecraft 28
Shikibu, Murasaki 6–7
songs 17, 22–23, 28
stories 4–5, 7, 10–11, 17–19, 22, 28–30

READ MORE

Leibowitz, Jean and Lisa LaBanca Rogers. *Discover Her Art: Women Artists and Their Masterpieces.* Chicago: Chicago Review Press, 2022.

Rose, Rachel. *Dolly Parton: Singer and Cultural Icon (Bearport Biographies).* Minneapolis: Bearport Publishing Company, 2023.

Shepherd, Crown. *Changemakers in the Arts and Literature: Women Leading the Way (The Future Is Female).* Minneapolis: Lerner Publications, 2024.

LEARN MORE ONLINE

1. Go to **www.factsurfer.com** or scan the QR code below.
2. Enter "**Women in Arts**" into the search box.
3. Click on the cover of this book to see a list of websites.